Grieving the Loss of Someone Who Is Still Very Much Alive

R. Marít

DORRANCE PUBLISHING CO
EST. 1920
PITTSBURGH, PENNSYLVANIA 15238

Dorrance Publishing Co
585 Alpha Drive
Pittsburgh, PA 15238
Visit our website at www.dorrancebookstore.com

ISBN: 979-8-89127-882-0
eISBN: 979-8-89127-380-1

It's not a date unless I spill my water
Or drop my food on my lap
Or knock something off the table
Here I am spilling
This is me spilling
My entire soul out for you to read.

1.
Denial

9.1.22

You say, 'I've been doing really good.'
And listed off all the things you haven't been doing,
Like laying in your bed, eyes red and puffy
Snot falling from your nose.
You haven't been sick, it's been easy to eat
You've been working out, going out,
Seeing people you hadn't when we were together.

I smile for you, because I can't smile for me.
While you are thriving, I feel like I'm dying.
I lay in my bed, going through all of our notes and books.
I force myself to eat, even though the only thing I ever crave is
you.
I went out once, drank too much, called you seventeen times.
I'm grieving what feels like a lifetime worth of love
And somehow you're using it like a scoop of preworkout protein
powder.

I send you a sunset as we say our goodbyes,
However do not misunderstand, this is not a goodbye gift at all.
I hope you take this sunset and watch it whenever you can.

Watch her turn the sky red, like the color of my hair
Tints of orange and yellow highlights.
Hold the sunset for me
Until we meet again and watch it together.

I'm terrified of dementia.
My mind will slowly dissipate and wilt
Unlike the one rose you gave me that I let dry,
And froze it in time with resin.

I fear I'll always think I'm 20 again, loving by your side.
I fear for the rest of my life, I'll think I'm still with you.
My old, fragile heart cannot bear the weight of missing you
So the deteriorating mind will convince me that I'm not
And I will die happily in that illusion.

I know it's you
Because when I'm not with you,
I fear I'll spend the rest of my life searching for someone like you
And I will never be satisfied.

It's been four months and I still listen to love songs
And think about you in every lyric
Even the songs about two souls living happily ever after
Especially those ones.

"It won't hurt like this forever."

That's what I'm afraid of.
The pain is one of the few things I have left of you.
What happens when you forget what life is like with me?
Will you find another lover?

Eclipse

If I am the moon, you are the sun.
Our time right now is unaligned,
But it is destiny that we meet again
And the world will stare in awe
That the sun and moon are together once again.

I don't want to love you out of necessity,
I want to love you freely.

You deserve a love like that.

Tonight I will dream of your lips pressed between my collarbone
and my neck,
One hand moving swiftly down the curve of my waist
While the other wraps itself gently around my neck.

It is as though your kiss is the key to unlocking my soul
And it opens up only for you.

A Pretense from My Own Fears.

You may be a man of few words,
But I am a writer with so much to say.

I try to fill in the blanks where you keep silent
And I wondered, for so long, if you really loved me
Or were you just too afraid to be alone?

When we meet again,
I hope you tell me about the adventures you had
And the people you loved.
I hope to hear all about your excitement, your pain, what has
brought you joy
I hope to hear about it all.

When we meet again,
I hope to tell you about how I finally found peace
Maybe we'll talk about what it was like,
The time you visited and we played a game of "War"
We laughed so hard I cried.

I'll leave out the part where I haven't laughed that hard since.

If I ever give love another chance
And he doesn't open the car door for me
I'm turning around and walking away.

If he doesn't tell me he still gets nervous
And blushes when he calls me pretty,
I'm not giving him the time of day
If he isn't anything like you.

2.
Anger

When you're young,
You worry about the monsters that come only at night.
Adults tell you there is no such thing as a monster under your bed
Or in your closet.
And now we sleep, trusting, while the monster lays next to us.

The pain I felt,
That ache for my own healing touch,
I hated it.
I despised it.
I tried so desperately to swallow it down,
Keep it from coming up,
Because if it did
It meant I'd have to walk away from the closest thing to love
And the closest person to family
I've ever known.

I would have let the fire consume me
As long as it was our house, together
That was burning to the ground.

It's a blessing to feel everything so deeply.
The wind doesn't just blow, it dances through my hair
The sun doesn't just shine, it twinkles off each dew-glazed blade of
grass.
The flowers don't just bloom, they stretch
and reach for the sake of the circle of life.

And it's a curse to feel everything so deeply.
The world doesn't just turn, sometimes it spins so fast I find
myself crashing to the ground as though I'm a crater colliding with
the moon.
The storm isn't just loud, it shakes the entire house while frames
fall and shatter to the ground.
The frost isn't just chilly, it suffocates my lungs and I can taste the
blood in the back of my throat.

You can tell them how you trusted me with the key to your heart
That I took it, and that to you it felt
like I threw it into the middle of the ocean
Leaving your heart open, and I bank robbed it.

But you cannot honestly say that I did not love you.

You know my reasons.

I think I am the way I am because
During those years
(The ones that are supposed to be the time of your life),
I spent grieving my childhood, and how it came crashing down
In a way that very few can understand.
I spent it grieving my innocence, and
How it was taken from me before I could give it up.
I spent those years being afraid, on edge, constantly trying
to prepare myself for the next big hit.

And now that I'm an adult, I'm still grieving
Walking through life with a hyperactive sense of awareness.
I'm grieving the years I never got because I was too deep in my
own head.
I'm grieving the needs that were often overlooked
The importance of the bare necessities of soft, gentle love.
I'm even grieving the years I spent grieving.

Someone asked me what I was afraid of once.
I love heights, and the ocean fascinates me.
I once tried to pull a snake free from an outdoor sticky-trap
in my dad's yard with my bare hands.
I go storm chasing in my car, and used to watch
Paranormal Activity in the mornings before school.
I sleep in the pitch dark,
Allowed a spider to live rent-free in my bathroom in the basement.

I do hate maggots, millipedes and centipedes,
But more than that, I fear one day I'll be scrolling on my phone
On the verge of falling asleep

And I scroll to a post
And it's you and a woman
And her ring finger sparkles as I see the two of you
And you just made the biggest promise to her.

The time between scrolling and seeing
Still, like the quiet before a storm.

"I can't imagine a day where I won't be angry," I began to say.
Then, my mind wandered to you.
The day I am no longer angry will be the day we meet again, and I
will understand that all this pain, all this growth, all this sacrifice
was worth it.

But until then, I will look up at the sky and scream until my lungs
give out
Because that is how much I have felt for you.

And I will curse the heavens for my torment,
That which resulted in our demise

And I will have this fire in my soul
That has nowhere to go since we've parted ways

Except for the pages of this book.

My life sometimes feels like one endless cycle of grief.
You know what that does to a person?
It either turns you into a monster
Or it turns you into the person you needed the most.

Either way, it kills the person you were
And I grieve for her, too.

I became drained from pulling you inside out,
Trying to get you to express how you felt
When you were sad, hurting, low
I would always know
But you'd never talk to me about it.

The problem with me having to pull it out of you
Was that I didn't know if you truly loved me
Or if you became comfortable and starting going through the motions
Thinking I wouldn't notice the effort that slowly slipped
As our time together went on.

I felt kept in the dark sometimes,
And you knew that
Because I told you in more ways than one.

"If they wanted to stay, they would."

Bullshit.
I wanted to stay so bad.
I wanted to feel safe and be around you all the time

I wanted to wake up to a post-it note sitting on my phone
In the mornings you had to leave to go somewhere before I was up.

I wanted us to cook together in the kitchen we shared
You cook the meat, I'll mix the guacamole and set the table
You heat up the tortillas, I'll fix us a vodka cocktail.

I wanted us to come home drunk and in love
And you'd sweep me up off my feet
and carry me past our dining room table.

I realized my breath was slowly turning toxic
And I was the chemical compound that was poisoning us.
Stepping away was the biggest and most challenging
proof of love I have ever done.

It was the hardest thing I have ever done in my entire life.

And I did it to save myself
And to protect you
Even though I so desperately wanted to stay.

I have always felt things so intensely.

When I paint, my first brush stroke violently strikes the canvas
If the bristles were sharp, the entire fabric would tear.

When I first learned how to climb trees,
I didn't stop at the first limb.
I climbed until I could see the sunset.

I have this terrible habit of submerging myself into a body of water
Without dipping my toes in first.

My spirals are more like atomic bombs.
The strength of the blast inside me,
All I want to do is push those closest to the epicenter
As far away as I possibly can.

People can't fix other people's problems
So instead, I fear that if I don't implode
The ones I love would just sit and watch me burn
While telling me they're here for me

Simply just being there doesn't do so much
When they can't possibly understand
What touching the sky feels like
And at the moment you feel like you'll be up there forever
You come crashing down from the height.

You think you're holding an unloaded gun,
But in reality you're holding a lighter
That sits right beside a line of gunpowder
Leading to dynamite.

You think it's just a joke
But it's far more than that.

"Love is not always kind."

Maybe if I was taught that it could be kind,
Things would have been different.

Maybe I wouldn't have almost thought that the boy
Who sulked in the corner until I
allowed my body to submit to his every wish
Loved me.

Maybe I wouldn't have almost thought that the boy
Who planned out the beginning of a new relationship
before ours ever ended
Loved me.

Maybe I wouldn't have almost thought that the boy
Who spoke of another woman between breaths
as he kissed me
Loved me.

Maybe I wouldn't have almost thought that the boy
Who wanted to be with me only when he was with someone else
Loved me.

Maybe I wouldn't have almost thought that the boy
Who kept pushing back plans until he finally left me
Loved me.

Maybe I wouldn't have almost thought that the boy
Who invited me into the back of his car in a Target parking lot
Loved me.

Maybe I wouldn't have almost thought that the boy
Who shoved his fingers down my throat to test my gag reflex
In a room surrounded by other men
Loved me.

Maybe I wouldn't have almost thought that the boy
Who grabbed my prepubescent breasts suddenly at recess
Loved me.

Maybe I wouldn't have almost thought that the boy
Who told me he got made fun of for talking to me
Loved me.

Maybe I wouldn't have almost thought that the boy
Who respected my bodily autonomy only when I was awake
Loved me.

Maybe I wouldn't have almost thought that the boy
Who only showed up when he wanted something
Loved me.

If I had been taught that love was supposed to be
Kind,
Respectful
Gentle
And patient
Maybe I wouldn't have pushed away the ones that were.

It affected me so much
That I couldn't sleep next to the one man I trusted with my entire life
Without swallowing two different sleeping pills
Before climbing into bed.

It affected me so much
That I no longer believe people are inherently good.

It affected me so much
I've been afraid to be single
Because men seem to only respect you
When another man holds claim over you.

Everyone says I've been handling this well,
That since I've been letting myself feel it all
And be upset
That I've been doing it right

What they don't realize
Is how tired I am of feeling so angry
At everything
And everyone
All the time.

And damn you.
There's a footprint you left on my wall from when you moved out
Scratches in the hallway that I will have to pay for
Images of us removed in less than four hours
While the one that you knew
would dig deep into my soul remained
—An alliance with a man that killed the girl that I was.

I never wanted war.

3.
Bargaining

I hadn't prayed in two years
Until I began to grieve the life I shared
With someone who is very much still alive.

It's funny, the lengths we go to when we're desperate.
Maybe if I prayed all along, our story would be different.

But maybe,
Just maybe
Because I started again,
Our story will end differently

I should have shown you all the poems I wrote about you,
All the journal excerpts where I described every little detail
About how loving you feels like a sunset,
You don't want to change a sunset's colors
You let it shine, and throughout all levels of the sky
Stare in awe at its effortless beauty.

I should have spoken to you the way I write about you.

If I had all the money in the world,
I would buy Paris, just so you could have it.
If that wasn't enough,
I would buy all of France
And if that still wasn't enough,
I would sell my soul so you could have the entire Universe.

I have ached and cried, turned my longing into verse
Written, and published words
In hopes that they reach you

I will do it over and over again
If that's what it takes to make you feel the love.

If it's another woman, I hope she makes you happy
Even though she won't write you poems
Or take brushstrokes across the canvas to remind you that you are loved,
That you are an entire galaxy.

She probably won't need constant reassurance,
But she also won't rip out her soul
And put it on a piece of paper
And write about your smile,
your two front teeth
The meaning of each of your tattoos
Your lips
The one curl that falls into the front of your face and
How it dangles just over your right eyebrow.

She probably won't feel things quite so deeply,
But she won't write about your hands
How you pick at your fingernails until they bleed
How you struggle with self-image even though you look like a sculpture
That only Michael Angelo could ever chisel out.
Your muscles, how they ripple all the way down your arms
Like thunder clouds, I suppose.

She probably won't carry a heavy weight of her past,
But she won't value the future the same way because of it
She won't look at the stars ever and pray that everything does happen
for a reason
She won't know when you first got the tattoo that says that
And the importance each artwork of ink in your skin has to you and
your story.

You don't deserve a half-wilted rose
That sells for the same price as a fully bloomed bouquet.

I hope I am just as accepted when I've bloomed
As I was when I was wilting.

If I ever have a daughter
After turning the pages of my scrapbook from a time when I was
young,
She will ask about love.

I will choke on my own words.

How will I tell her that with great love comes great pain,
And the world is a terrifying place
Where many soulmates only stay for a chapter?

We'll sit on the porch of our home,
Two rocking chairs and nothing but a table and an ashtray between us.

"We're visiting the grandkids tomorrow," I'll remind you.

You'll smile as you pass me the smoke in your old, frail hand
And I'll reach for it as my wrinkled fingers tremble.
We are wise and at peace, finally.

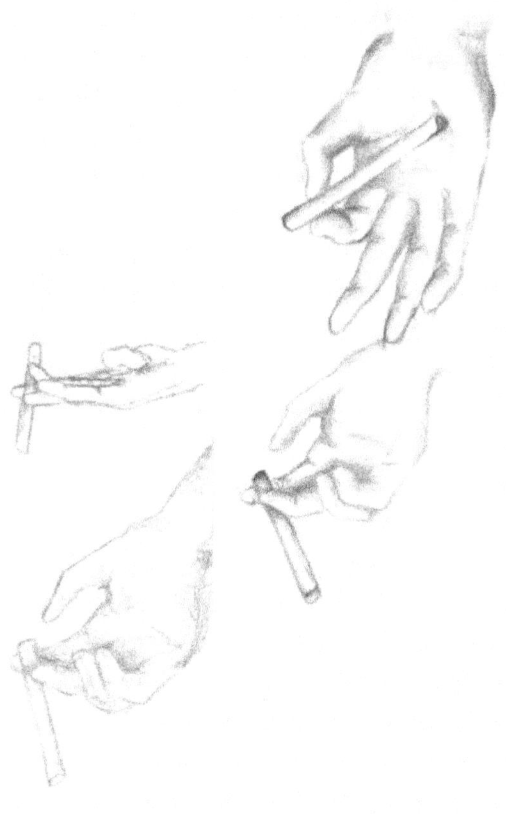

4.
Depression

I understand if you try to hate me.
It's harder to move on when you end on good terms.
But I will love you,
I will only speak of you in the highest sense
As the love we had slips from my tongue

And when somebody asks why we are no longer
I will look down at my wrist where a silver bracelet used to sit,
Sometimes still sits,
And I will smile at the memories that flash by,
"Right person, wrong time."

I dumped out my wine last night,
Watched it swirl down the drain of ~~our~~ my kitchen sink.
At one point, I lay quivering on ~~our~~ my bathroom floor,
Staring up at the two emerald green towels that hung from a rack.
My blurry gaze shifted to the hook behind the bathroom door
Where your graduation cap and gown should have been hanging.

I fell asleep in your gaming chair last night
Curled up in between the cushioned arms.
They were the closest thing to feeling
like I was being held by you again.

Your clothes remain in your designated closet,
Your hats still perch on the wall.
The ghost of you haunts me every night,
And it kills me to know you're living a different life.

I wonder if my cat knows that you're gone.

I hope you do heal
And I hope you experience a life full of joy
And lessons
And love

But selfishly, deep down inside
I hope you miss me
Until you don't have to anymore
Whatever outcome that may be

I didn't cry for the first four hours I woke up.
That's the easy part, though.

The real challenge is going out;
Choking back the tears every time I pass an apartment we looked at,
Or a restaurant we dined together in,
Or the cuisine I know you love.

I told a mutual friend about a restaurant I knew you'd love.
I hope they took you there, and you enjoyed it.

I didn't cry for the first four hours I woke up.

"There's no such thing as right person, wrong time."

Says the person who has never experienced
What it's like to have your whole life crashing down on you
While you have no capacity to give what the person you love
Deserves

Because you're young
And haven't learned how to learn to be on your own
And mend your own wounds
Without taking the ones you love down in the process.

There are days where I swear I can still feel you.
I go to a coffee shop and resist the urge to buy your coffee
The way you used to get it with almond milk.
You'd get it that way so I could have a taste,
Without my stomach aching
Even though you already bought me my own.

You were always doing that;
Making sure I had enough to eat,
Making sure that, just in case I wanted to try your food,
You'd get it without the ingredients I couldn't eat.
Do you ever still do that?

I spilled popcorn kernels all over my sink
And I laughed, imagining how it would go if you were here.
I'd hear you chuckling at the fact that
I am the clumsiest person we both know,
But it was one of your favorite things about me.

It was really painful, hearing the kernels pop
Because you are not laughing with me on a Thursday night
When we both stayed in to make popcorn and
Watch a cop chase online, sitting on our couch.

I am sitting alone, living alone, with only the sound of kernels
To fill the emptiness that has only grown louder since you've been gone.

Every time I think I'm done writing sorrowful poems of us
I see an image of you
And I wonder if I'll ever be able to look at you
Without feeling this ache deep beneath the skin of my chest
Like you're still a part of me.

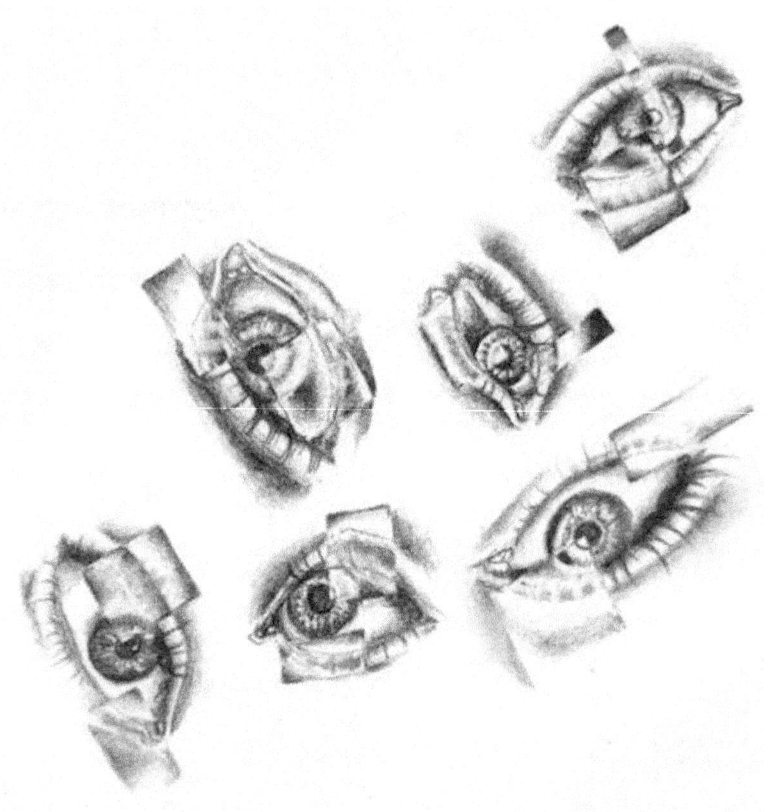

Missing you is what I imagine pain, if it were an animal, to feel like.
It sinks its talons deep into my chest,
Piercing my heart,
My body trapped,
paralyzed in its teeth.

Right here is where you decide that you no longer miss me,
And for some twisted reason my mind cannot logically come to
that conclusion.
I will spend the rest of my life in some sort of delusion.

I've been howling at the moon.
The wind blows by as it takes my cries with it.
I wonder if you can hear them.
I wonder if you can feel them.

Tu Me Manques

French is the language of love,
And I've never heard something that quite encapsulates how I feel.

The French do not say "I miss you."
Instead, they say Tu Me Manques
"I am missing from you."

I feel like I'm dying
Were the words that came out of my mouth.
I guess in a way, I was dying.
A part of me was dying, only it wasn't death by gunshot.
No.
This was slow and painful.
The kind of pain where you can't breathe for weeks
And your chest aches
And you feel like unzipping your own skin
And crawling out of it.

And when I accept the reality that I will always carry love for you
Together or apart,
Do I put that in the depression category of grief,
The denial category of grief,
Or the acceptance part of grief?

I set wildflowers on the window outside the movie theater.

It felt like I was visiting our grave.

Today was the first day I didn't wake up crying for you.
Overall, it was the first day I didn't shed a tear
And somehow, that felt worse
Because even though my body won't produce tears,
My heart is torn.

The psychologist told me that the pain I feel now will subside
That the mind and body work hard to return to homeostasis.
She said it's not physically sustainable to feel this pain,
So our body reacts and overtime will adapt.

Imagine a heartbreak so strong
That your mind and body must work so hard
Just to survive.

My thumb hovers over the "share" button on my phone
Muscle memory.
Even my fingers haven't gotten over you.

I vomited in the sink that was supposed to be our sink,
Went to cry in the king sized bed that was supposed to be our bed.
Felt sick again,
Vomited in the toilet that, if you were still here,
you'd probably forget to close the lid of
It was like my body was going through withdrawals.
Everything in my entire being, ached.

The last night before you moved all your things out,
I must confess I fell asleep on the couch your mom gave us.

I put on your gaming headset for a couple of seconds,
Just to feel close to you.

I sat in your closet and cried,
Surrounded by your smell.

I put on one of your favorite sweatshirts and fell asleep in your clothes,
Yet another night in a row.

I fought hard against rest and refused to close my eyes
until I couldn't fight it anymore.
I didn't want to waste any time being asleep
When I could be spending the last few hours
surrounded by what was left of you.

I've been oversleeping a lot lately,
But my body doesn't feel tired at all.
I think it's my heart that's exhausted.

When you moved out,
You left all the things you knew I loved.

You left me your glass table I used for my artwork,
You left me your TV with the networking still connected,
You left me the blanket your mom gave us when we first moved in,
You left me the cute salt and pepper shakers
that sat on our dining room table,
You left me a candle wick cork,
You left me your plates,
You left me your spices,
You left me the bread knife,
You left me the cutting boards,
And you left me your bear.

That speaks volumes to the kind of man you are.

I think the saddest type of breakups
Are the ones where you don't want to leave
But you know you have to
If you want to get your own head above water.

It's been almost five months and
The longer I go without you feels like the longer I go without air.
It's supposed to get better.
I miss you terribly.

Lately I've been having trouble sleeping
I wake up sad, thinking
Here goes another day

Except for the mornings I wake up with a smile on my face
And I'm confused at first,
But then realize it's because I dreamt of you all night

I've been dreaming a lot about you recently
And about us finding each other again
I'm happy to see you in my dreams
I'm happy to feel your arms wrap around my body again
I'm happy to touch your face, twirl my fingers around your curls
I'm happy to hear your voice

Even if it's for a fleeting moment
Even if waking up ruins the rest of my day.

A mosquito bit my cheek
It reminded me of you, your lips pressed there
I have an itch for you
Yet it is one I just can't seem to scratch.

You can delete the photos of us.
You can burn everything I gave to you
And if that helps you heal, I hope you do.

But I will still be there in memory.
I will still be there in the smoke
From the burning books I gave you for each year we were together.
I will be there in the scar I left on your heart,
The scar which I will spend forever trying to atone for.

Anyone who has experienced your love
Has experienced a taste of heaven
For it is so pure,
So kind,
So gentle and genuine

It's hard to believe your love can exist in this cruel world.

I can't cry.
I'm still so sad, but the tears aren't coming.
It appears my heart isn't the only thing experiencing a drought.
I think my mind hurts so bad that it's blocking it all out,
But I can still feel it.
I can still feel it so deeply.

The ache.

I've written our wedding vows,
"Goodbye" notes,
Eulogies,
Letters I've burnt until there was nothing left but ash.
I write with deep passion
But nothing has come close
To the words I wish I could say to you right now.

I not only miss my lover,
I miss my best friend.

I miss laughing on my bed at midnight
Before we bought a bigger one together
And created too much space between us.

I want to gossip with you,
Tell you something about someone
That I know would make you laugh
And only you would understand it.

It's ironic
There is nothing poetic about losing you,
There is no metaphor that can perfectly encapsulate
The emptiness reflected in our apartment
that I felt deep within my soul.
There is nothing poetic about the gut wrenching,
Mind crushing,
Aching pressure in my chest.

I look for you in the background of photos your friends post
It worries me when you're not in them
I hope you're okay

"Bus driver arrested on DUI charge
while driving Pirates from Chicago to Milwaukee."

The heartbreak hurt so bad I started
obsessively reading the news as a distraction.
I wanted to read something that wasn't poetic.
Something that wasn't about how in losing you
I lost a part of myself
But written like it was a beautiful thing to happen.
Something that wasn't about one of the biggest tragedies in my life
But written like it wasn't.

I know it's silly
But sometimes I still think I'll wake up one morning and
This whole year will have been just a dream.
I'm not sure why but it's really difficult for my mind to
Comprehend that things in real life can get this bad and this dark
That someone can feel this sad,
Yet manages to wake up every day to feed the cat,
Put gas in her car and drive to work.

I fear that some day my daughter
will look back at the scrapbook I made
Or find the photo books of us that I will never throw away.
I fear she will ask who the man is
that's kissing me under the blue fireworks.
What am I supposed to tell her?

Sometimes it feels like I can't let myself feel it all, you know?
I worry that if I let it all flood in, it will take a hold of me.
My darkest hours are incredibly atramentous.

The minute I let it all in,
I have to do it alone because,
For someone else to see me that way,
Can be like inhaling the smoke from a raging fire.

Loving you is like learning how to ride a bike.
I can't unlearn it, even when there is no bicycle.
I can't unlearn what it's like to love you, even when you're gone.

In the midst of pictures popping up with a "swipe left or right"
prompt
I got lost in swiping left repeatedly
Over and over again
Left
Left
Left
Until I realized I was only searching for you.

"No you don't understand," she cried out
"He was my family.
He knew more about me than anyone.
He was my future."

How could anyone possibly understand
That someone can be all those things
And you can still not be strong enough,
Ready enough,
For any of it.

"Real love knows when to say goodbye."

I would have rather died than cut our tie
And that's exactly the problem
I was dying.

I lay on the bathroom floor,

I felt like calling you, I was in so much pain
But if you answered I know what would have happened.
You'd come running, swooping in to save me,
Just like you've done a thousand times before
but in many different ways.
I couldn't be selfish.
It was your night, a night you should be celebrating.

I moved my hand to the toilet lever,
Gave it a flush
Didn't dial your number,
Dragged myself up off the cold tile,
Threw on some pajamas and put myself to bed.
The next day I emptied out all the liquor on the shelf.
The sink drank every last drop.

Don't you see? This is what I have to learn to do on my own.

5.
Acceptance

Every once in a while
I hear the voice inside of me yell
"I'm done."

She is so tired, but she's never actually finished.
She picks herself up
Every single time.

What I said that day, I meant most of it
The part where I don't know how to stand on my own two feet
And that I have to figure out how to walk before I am able to run
Give them the full strength of love like they deserve.

What I regret is saying that we made a mistake.
We never made a mistake.
I'm so thankful for every hour,
Every minute,
Every moment I spent with you.

Even if that's all I'll ever have now.

When someone asked about you
I spoke about how you changed my life.
I spoke about how high you set the bar,
How deeply we cared for each other.

Even though I heard the names you called me after it was over
Felt the dirt you rubbed on my name
Smelled the shit you made up to make yourself feel better

Yet I still speak of you highly anyways
Because I know you so deeply
This is how you've always coped with the loss of someone you love
I forced us both to grieve
I could never hate you for the ways you tried to pull yourself back
together.

If I had one glass of water
And was dying of thirst
And you were a tiny little succulent cactus
I would give you all of the water in my cup
Not knowing that you didn't need all of it
And that I should never give my life,
Pouring everything that I am
For a soul that can persevere on its own

Learning to keep what I need

There is no greater love
Than protecting someone when you know you need to do better.

When you walk away while being very much still in love,
You risk everything that matters.

The time it takes to do better,
Even when you have hope that your stars will align,
You risk losing that person forever
To someone else
With the knowledge that if someone else makes them happier
It's okay.

It might kill, but when you love them so deeply
So intensely,
All you've ever wanted is to see them succeed.

I didn't even know it was possible to ever love someone this much.

It's vital to know how to swim in deep waters
Before jumping on a boat
The same way it is essential to know yourself
Before you share your essence with someone else.

All I know is that if my heart breaks at the hands of another,
I will be okay.
Not because I've moved on,
But rather a burning bridge is no threat to someone who can swim.

I will learn to save myself from drowning.

I wanted acceptance to look something like
Going into Starbucks and not thinking of your order,
Buying groceries, skipping over the dairy aisle
And not wondering if you found a cheese you like yet.

I wanted acceptance to look something like
Running my hands through someone else's hair
And not twirling my fingers around the curls that aren't theirs
Not searching for the birthmark that isn't there.

I wanted acceptance to look something like
Sitting on the balcony that used to be ours
And not looking for your Nissan passing by.
Not hoping that it will, either.

Instead, acceptance looks something like
Someone asking about you
And I describe how wonderful we were
And I let it hurt because that was the past.

Acceptance looks something like
Knowing that there will always be a part of you
That resides in my heart
And even if I'd prefer you in your fullness
I will be okay if that is all I will ever have
Because I have my own heart.

I am a lover of words,
You are a man of few.

You taught me that words don't need to be spoken
In order to love.
In fact, you taught me that love is in the action,
Something I never knew before I experienced loving you.

I'm learning how to let myself cry.
It's such a weird thing,
Having to teach yourself as an adult that it's okay to feel your emotions
That it's okay to sob when you're going through a loss
It's okay to weep when your heart aches.

I see the girls with bright eyes, wide smiles, bodies swaying
As they fall into the dancing crowd,
and I wish I was someone else for the night.
For a split second do I wish I had never met you,
only so I can forget what it feels like to have lost you.

And then I remember how lucky am I
To have experienced a love that most of these people have not,
To feel your arms around my waist,
your breath against my neck,
your fingers on my lips.
How lucky am I to experience what it feels like to be loved by you.

Learning that sometimes people grow apart and
Relationships are often temporary but
You can never get rid of the roots from someone you grew with
At some point they had intertwined with your own and
Even as you grow apart
There will always be that link.

I move forward now with my life
And rather than spend my nights trying to cut you away
I am thankful for the time we grew together and
I would never trade it for the world.
You'll always have a part of me with you.

You can't stay hooked up to an IV forever.
At some point, you will be discharged
And your body will have to learn to replenish itself on its own.

I can't wait for the day where my body learns how to restore what it lost,
Where it learns how to recover from whatever broke inside of it.

You've got to stop digging your misery down so deep
Just to avoid hurting people that wouldn't think twice
about hurting you if it came down to it.
You've got to stop overstaying your welcome
just because you're afraid of being alone.
You've got to stop making people your home
As long as you allow someone to hold that power,
They will burn you up from the inside out.

They say to heal what hurt you
Or you'll bleed on the people that didn't cut you
And darling,
You are covered in my blood.

It's time I get the bleeding under control,
Stitch my own wounds and clean my bandages
And heal.

When I came crumbling down,
I wanted to rebuild the same structure of who I was before
Rather than adapt.

But we cannot survive in an environment
For long periods of time
Unless we can learn how to adapt.

My heart beats, and I will fight until I consistently want to keep it
that way
Until the pounding in my chest feels good
and is content with the sound of itself.

When your heart beats, I hope it makes you feel proud of how far
you've come.
All the pain this world has brought you,
and here you are, beating in spite of it all.

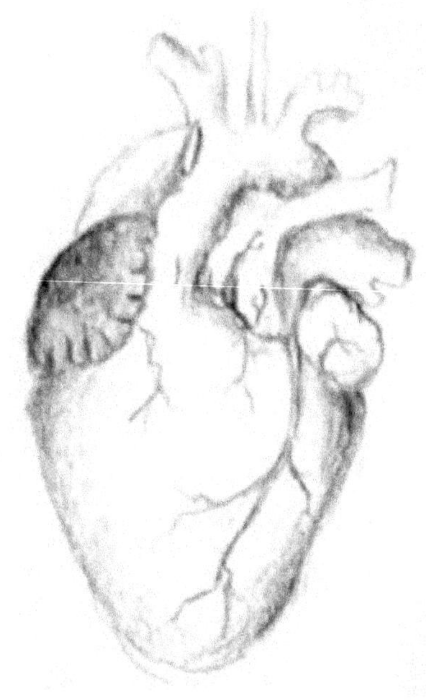

I think it's so interesting how a drastic change in appearance
Often symbolizes a drastic change in oneself.
As I look back over the last couple years, I see a slow change
The type of change that you don't notice every day
Not even every month
But when you step back, you can see how the person I was
To the person I am now
Look and feel nothing alike.

And I'm proud of who I've become.

I had this image of myself before a lot of things happened.
At one point, I tried everything I could to become her.
If I couldn't feel like her, maybe I could look like her.
I ended up succeeding and doing both.
It was only then, however, that I recalled how truly sad I was.

In life, there is no going backwards.

I don't recognize anything in my life anymore
And I'm still trying to decide if that's a terrible thing
Or a beautiful blessing.

An ode to myself

I have always felt as though my purpose on this earth is to love.
I haven't always been very good at it,
But I've always tried.

I have so much love in my heart
It used to be so overwhelming
When I felt as though I had nobody to give it to.

I realized the love in my heart
Is needed most
Exactly there
In my heart.

You were wrong.
I am not chaos.
I have chaos, I feel chaotic,
But I am not what I have nor what I feel.

I am also gentle
The smell of wet grass after a thunderstorm,
A light brush stroke on a canvas,
The fingers that graze the soft top of my cat's head.

I am learning how to hug again,
How to not feel ashamed by the fact
That sometimes I like the tenderness,
And sometimes the chaos hurts.

What I've learned so far
Is that at the end of every episode,
I am the only person picking up my naked body from the floor of
the shower.
I am the only person bandaging my wounds,
Washing my feet in the bathtub after walking home alone barefoot,
Feeding myself when I had neglected myself,
Moving my clothes from the washing machine to the dryer,
Pouring bottles of whiskey down the sink.

It's me.
I'm the one.

I'm learning how to take care of myself
And I enjoy it

But that doesn't mean I don't miss
the way you kissed me where it hurt.

The most important lesson I've learned when it comes to friendships,
Is when people tell you their negative traits
Believe them.

Do not waste your time trying to convince them they are being
hard on themselves
And that they are not a narcissist, they just put themselves first
All the time
Recklessly
No matter who gets hurt
For their own benefit.

They know themselves better than you ever will.

I wonder if my cat can tell that I'm healing.

When he's hungry in the mornings,
I make myself breakfast to eat with him.
When he's hungry at night,
I pull out my popcorn machine and we share a snack.
He gets more treats now, little bits of the food I've eaten
throughout the day.
I don't lock him out of the bathroom when I cry.
Instead, I'll pick him up, set him on my lap,
He'll nudge me with his little furry head
So as to say, "This is a nice change."

I go back and forth between writing about wanting you back
And learning to accept that sometimes characters stay for just a
few chapters.
I don't think the effect you left could ever dissipate in just a few
chapters.

Hearing that "if it's meant to be, it will"
But wondering how many times in this life does the right pair split,
Never to find each other again for all the wrong reasons?

You are the strongest love I have known,
And often I wonder is it the strongest love I will ever know,
Or will there be a love out there that is strong in different ways?

Will I find you again, years from now
Or will I spend more of my life missing you
Than I have loving you?

The unknown has become more of a comfort than a fear lately
Until it comes down to you,
I don't want any of my fears to ever touch you.

No matter what happens, what our futures look like,
I will never want anything to ever harm you
And that is the only thing I know for sure.

Growth

I'm scrolling on my phone as I make breakfast.
It's 8:43 am, I just woke up.
It was a picture of her.
My knees were taken out from beneath me.
I fell to the floor clenching my chest.

The breath in my lungs had been vacuumed out
By the cruelty of what it means to love someone.

I did not break the plate you left me before you moved out.
I did not throw my phone at the wall where your shoe print still is.
I finished making breakfast despite the sick churning in my stomach.
I wanted to resort to old habits, but I promised I'd heal.

So instead,
I told her to take care of you,
And that you deserve nothing short of the world.

Did she tell you that?

Is this what it means to know that you have truly loved someone?

Ah, and I guess you will read all these words
And wonder
"If you loved him so much, why did you go?"

The answer is simple.
A man like that deserves the entire world
And I could not give that to him yet

Not while my world was on fire
Not while my hands were burning
Not while I had no idea how to help myself.

I am scavenging the continents and putting out my fires.
Hopefully he will find his own flames to put out, too.

If he is still there, and our hearts fly into each other,
The time between then and now will have all been worth it
And we will not burn, we will have adapted to the change.

In the chance we do not find each other,
Perhaps we will be two strangers in love with someone else
And if that is what makes us truly happy, then I have set us both free.

Free either way.

To the Reader,

I encourage you to live a life unchained.
Run at the speed of wind,
Follow your heart.
You deserve nothing less than the best version of anyone.
Do not settle.
Do not expect anyone to have life figured out, especially right now.
Do not listen to that critical voice in your head
that tells you that you're not enough,
I remember how rude it is to you.
You are more than enough.
You always have been.
You are so important that I have written an entire book for you,
And I will keep writing you books if that's what it takes to quiet
the critic
Even just a little bit
For *you.*